the DOUBLE DOOR Inn

Est. 1973

Written by Debby Wallace
Photographs and editing by Daniel Coston
Interviews conducted by Debby Wallace and Daniel Coston
Designed by Adam Roth

Our thanks to all those whose stories and photographs are featured in the book, and to Adam Roth for his time and work on this book. Special thanks to Nick Karres, the Karres family, and everyone that works at the Double Door Inn.

CHARLOTTE'S HOME OF THE BLUES:
40 Years Of the Double Door Inn

Fort Canoga Press
fortcanogapress.blogspot.com
FCP-002

Portions of this book were originally published in Home Of The Blues: 35 Years Of The Double Door Inn, by Outskirts Press in 2009. Our thanks to Outskirts Press for their support.

PRINTED IN THE UNITED STATES OF AMERICA

CHARLOTTE'S
HOME OF THE BLUES

∽ 40 YEARS OF ∽
THE DOUBLE DOOR INN

Fort Canoga Press

THANKS

Our thanks to the following people, whose purchase of a special edition copy helped to fund the making of this book.

Keith Plyler
Shaun McDermott
Matthew Karres
Larry Lipscomb
Betsy Norton Stowe
Jeri Thompson
Jill & Mark Olson
Bob Nelson
Brian Dunn
Rita Miller
David & Kay Anderson
Richard Walt
Don Carras
Delta Moon
Janet & Don Profant
Michelle Mastenbrook
Rick Booth
Kelly Karres
Cole Karres
Larry Brundage
Phil Hensley
Michael Wallace
Molly & Dennis Coston
Dennis Kiel
Scott Benfield

*This book is dedicated to the entire family of Nick
and Matthew Karres, my children, Michael and Michelle,
and my mentor, Janine K.
–Debby Wallace*

*For Sandra, George & Mary King, Nick Karres and
everyone involved with the Double Door Inn story.
Thank you for 40 years of blood, sweat and beers.
–Daniel Coston*

NIGHTHAWKS ONSTAGE, 1978.
Courtesy Double Door Inn archives

CHARLOTTE'S HOME OF THE BLUES

~ 40 YEARS OF ~
THE DOUBLE DOOR INN

Nick Karres, the man that has managed the Double Door Inn for 40 years, once shared a quote that in it's simplicity, really says a lot. After talking with him about his business, being present for many of the great shows and coming to know a little more about how difficult sustaining such a business could be, I had to ask him the obvious question. Why would anyone spend their entire working life in a business that is challenging at it's best and quite miserable at it's worst? He looked thoughtful for just a moment and then said, "You either get it or you don't."

The Double Door Inn began as a small family endeavor that grew into a groundbreaking music venue. In 1973, when the business was first opened, there was not a single hint that one day, musicians like Delbert McClinton, Eric Clapton, Keb Mo, or Stevie Ray Vaughn would perform in the building that was originally erected in 1911 as a family residence on a gravel street, in what was then the outskirts of Charlotte, North Carolina.

Over the years, many things have changed yet sustaining the music that is categorized as the blues has quite a rich tradition in this country. Blues music has taken so many forms that it is difficult to describe simply. It has often been said that when you hear the blues, you will know it. That is most likely a fair statement. Through ups and downs, having commercial success or not, the music has endured. In that way, the subject of this work is quite similar to the blues in that as a business establishment, it has also endured.

NICK KARRES, MID 1970s.
Courtesy Double Door Inn archives

The most important thing about blues music is that it evokes emotions with often simple stories as well as a distinctive beat. Some would argue that blues music began with W.C. Handy and his early compositions. Others believe that it began at the crossroads in the Delta when Robert Johnson, the story goes, sold his soul to the devil. Some believe that the blues died with Stevie Ray Vaughn. But the blues, like many other forms of music, lives on in those who continue to enjoy it, and the places where it finds a home.

The Double Door Inn in Charlotte, North Carolina, located in the same location with the same ownership and management, has earned the Double Door the distinction of being the second oldest such place in the United States. The building still stands in the same location, even though its street name has been changed. From the outside, there is nothing to indicate that there is anything special on the inside. The building is two stories high and has two front doors. Only one of the doors is operable. The plate glass windows are smudged and there is a blue neon sign that advertises "Live Blues."

Once you enter the establishment, it may take a little time to realize just what an unusual place you have entered. The lighting is dim and there is nothing glittery about the surroundings. The wooden floors may look dirty. Everything inside definitely has some age on it. But don't be fooled. This is a place with a history that is almost unbelievable and an ambiance that can sometimes feel like a church for those who are fans of blues music. To those who take the time to look at all of the pictures of past performers that surround the walls, it is obvious that this is the real deal. This is definitely a blues joint. Look up at the old wooden rafters of what was at one time an actual family residence. The bar is wooden, the floors are wooden and there are stools at the bar that are also wooden. There are advertisements for various brands of beer. Behind the bar, there are shelves lined with bottles of different kinds of liquor. There are at least three clocks that are visible if one sits at the bar. The time is never the same on any of them. But no one had any idea that such a place would still exist in 2008 when it was opened on December 22, 1973.

In 1973, gasoline prices were quickly escalating and had hit $1.00 a gallon, the economy was in a recession, and the business climate was not very good. Interest rates were at a historic high. There was change in the air. A young Charlotte native, Nick Karres, not long past his graduation from UNC-Chapel

ORIGINAL SEATING AREA OF THE CLUB, MID 1970S.
Courtesy Double Door Inn archives

ORIGINAL FRONT AREA OF THE CLUB.
Courtesy Double Door Inn archives

Hill, was working for a local real estate company. With the economic conditions of the time, the job was a challenge. One of his assignments was to try and find a business to lease the building at 218 Independence Boulevard that had recently been vacated when the Peggy Houston Lamp Shop relocated.

According to Karres, "I kept trying to lease this building, but everything kept falling through. Interest rates made it difficult to find a business willing to lease the space. At the time, there were very few places in Charlotte where young people could go to hang out and perhaps drink a beer. So I began to consider opening a small bar in the building. My older brother, Matthew had some experience in the business so I consulted with him about the possibilities. I almost literally begged him to go into this business with me. I knew that I wanted a family member involved, should I start a business. Matthew Karres was at first reluctant. "I had worked in bars in Chapel Hill and Charlotte, but I was not sure that I wanted to be involved in actually owning such a business," says Matthew Karres today. "I had several concerns ranging from the actual location that Nick had in mind to whether or not we would be able to secure an ABC (Alcohol Beverage Control) permit to sell beer." But after much discussion about the possibilities, the brothers decided that they would open a small bar in the building.

It took some imagination to turn the old lamp shop into a bar. According to Matthew, "This building was originally a residence that was built in 1911 by the Wearn Lumber Company. At that time, it was located in the outskirts of Charlotte on a gravel road known as Fox Street."

By 1973, the road had become a major highway known then as Independence Boulevard, very near the center of the downtown district. Central Piedmont Community College was located just across the street. Behind the building, there was a nice size community where many younger people lived due to the low rents for apartments and houses, and the close proximity to the community college.

Since both of the Karres brothers were fairly recent college graduates, neither had a lot of money. Some startup capital was definitely needed. They discussed the situation with their parents, James and Georgia. "They were not really impressed with our idea," Nick remembers. "They had concerns about what problems we might encounter with such a business. Operating a business that served alcohol in the Bible belt was a somewhat radical idea at the time."

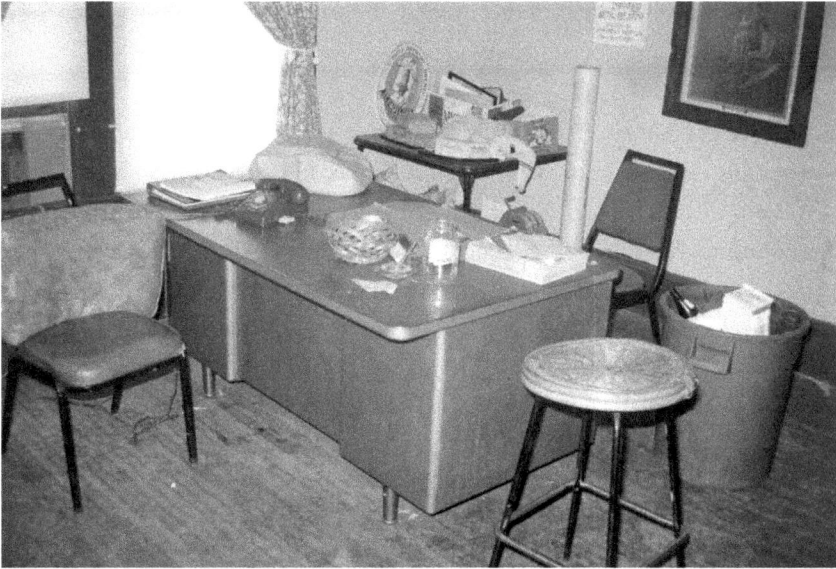

NICK KARRES' OFFICE, 1970s.
Courtesy Double Door Inn archives

GAME ROOM, 1970s.
Courtesy Double Door Inn archives

Eventually, however, their father agreed to loan them $10,000 to start the business.

Finding an appropriate name for the new business proved to be another detail that was of some initial concern. Most bars had themes and for a time, Nick considered a Western theme. He had seen a movie that had a bar called the Double Eagle. According to Matthew, "We went to the library and started checking phone books in Chicago, where we had relatives, and also New York City. I remember discussing our quandary one evening at dinner with our parents. Our mother looked thoughtful for a moment and then in a matter of fact way, said the place has two doors. 'Why don't you call it the Double Door?' This sounded logical to the two of us and resulted in us naming the business the Double Door Inn."

Renovations took about six months before the building was ready to operate as a bar. Initially the bar was quite small. "We just opened up as a bar with a jukebox and no thoughts at all of live music. We just opened as a place for people to come. Originally, the bar was quite small," Nick remembers. "Actually you could come into the bar, turn left and go through the kitchen, and be all the way around. When customers first entered, there was a large window that opened into the bar ."

One of the first official regulars at the bar was Travis, a Korean War veteran that lived nearby. During the first few years, he spent many an afternoon hanging around and expressing his opinion on just about everything as he sipped from a can of Pabst Blue Ribbon beer. He met a cook named Virginia, who was employed at a nearby restaurant and frequently walked with her to her job, and then back to the Double Door. When they decided to get married in late 1974, the natural place for the ceremony was the bar. Neil Hamlin, who had a mail order credential to practice as a minister, officiated at the ceremony. Later, there was a reception complete with wedding cake, and the event was covered by the Charlotte Observer, the first time that the local daily paper covered the still-fledgling bar.

This event was only one of the many things that made this destination special to many people. Stories abound of people who either met at the Double Door, played music there, or spent many years working to keep the business going. "If I had to hire, fire and continuously train employees, I wouldn't be able to get anything else done," shares Nick Karres. "These people have been a big factor in

PATRONS AT THE BAR, 1970s.
Courtesy Double Door Inn archives

ORIGINAL SPACE LEADING FROM BACK ROOM OF
DOUBLE DOOR INN. Courtesy Double Door Inn archives

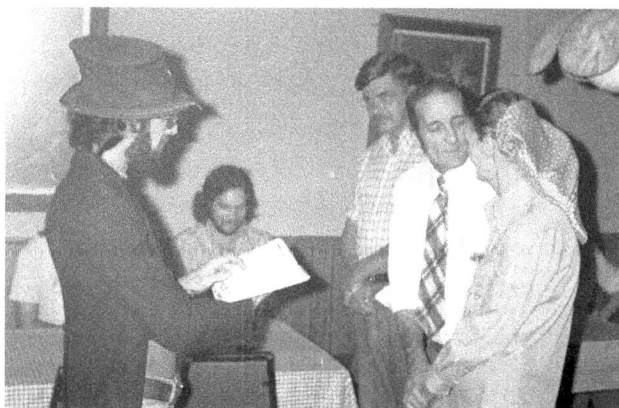

TRAVIS' WEDDING, 1975.
Courtesy Double Door Inn archives

allowing me to continue this business. When I m not here, they take care of the night business and look after things as well as they would if it were theirs. If I had a lot of employee turnover, I would have burned out a long time ago."

"As new bars began to open, I could see the fickle nature of the business," adds Nick. "We began to see that if we planned on being here for awhile, we needed to make a decision. Our need for something different to draw customers on a more regular basis coincided with the need for a place for local musicians to play."

Currently, at least one employee has been working for Karres for the past 33 years. Others have been employed for ten, fifteen or even twenty or more years. Mike Martin, night bartender, has been employed at the Double Door since 1975. "I began working on a part-time basis. I had been coming here as a customer frequently enough that I had gotten to know both Nick and Matt," says Martin. "One day, I happened to be around and heard someone mention needing to take some time off for vacation. Nick knew that I was working already part-time at the Yellow Rose Tavern so he asked me if I wanted to fill in. I took him up on the request and I have worked here ever since."

In the beginning, Martin worked in the kitchen when the venue used to sell pizza and had its own pizza oven. "Joe Smothers and I used to make and sell pizzas, box after box during that time, and then eventually, I also began working behind the bar slinging beers. As I began to get more hours here, this became my primary job."

He has several tales and legends from the past, but one of the most exciting was his recollection of being there when some of the true blues greats came in for a show. "I can remember especially when Luther Allison played here. The show started with his back-up band who played several numbers. Just as the crowd got a little restless, I heard an almost thunderous noise from the front staircase. I looked up and sure enough, here came Allison down the steps, playing his guitar and wandering through the packed crowd to the stage. Once he hit the stage, the band played straight through for more than two and a half hours. The audience didn't even ask for an encore. Everyone was so blown away by the show that they were almost stunned. I do remember the guys in the band had to almost run to the men's room. After sipping water all night and playing so long, they definitely had to go!"

MIKE (EMPLOYED SINCE 1975) TENDING BAR, JUNE 2008.
Photo by Daniel Coston

"Another great time was probably the only time that I have ever seen the Nighthawks play when I was not working. They were doing a grand opening at a place called Rosie's Cantina in Atlanta and had invited Nick to come down for the show. I went along with him. We had VIP seats, access to the band and everything. I remember the band put on a superior show and it was a great evening. All of our drinks were paid for but at exactly 4:00 AM, it was all over. The place was closing and the waitresses would not even give us a glass of water. We all had to go! We hooked up with the band, went somewhere for breakfast and then turned around and drove all the way back to Charlotte, having been up for over 24 hours. That was some night!"

When asked why he has stayed on and made the Double Door his career for 33 years, Martin offers a clear answer. "To me, Nick is one of the main reasons that I stuck around. No matter what things I might have done incorrectly, he always was there, and offered sometimes fatherly advice but because of him, it became worthwhile to stay. He was always fair in all of his dealings with me, and has always treated all of us with respect. He likes what he does even though he has quite a difficult job, but I am most appreciative of all the opportunities that I have had due to this job. I had the opportunity to later go on to UNCC and earn my B.A. degree and even took some graduate courses due to the flexible hours that I worked. When my son played T-ball and soccer, I was always there. I even had the time to coach some of his teams and had I been working more traditional hours, I would never have been able to have done all of those things as well as earn a living."

Of course, as with any job, there are things that are not always pleasant. "Probably the worst part of the job for me personally is dealing with patrons who may be very nice in the beginning of the evening. After they have a few drinks, personalities often change and the same person who was very nice and easy-going only two or three hours ago, may turn into an unpleasant, loud obnoxious person. I often have to remind myself that I have some complicity when this happens as I am the person who served them the alcohol. Sometimes, it is difficult to deal with their behavior, yet knowing that I was the one who served them, I have to stay in control of my own feelings. We are taught to watch customers for the signs of overindulgence but it can be very difficult to spot, especially on a busy evening when orders are coming in from all sides.

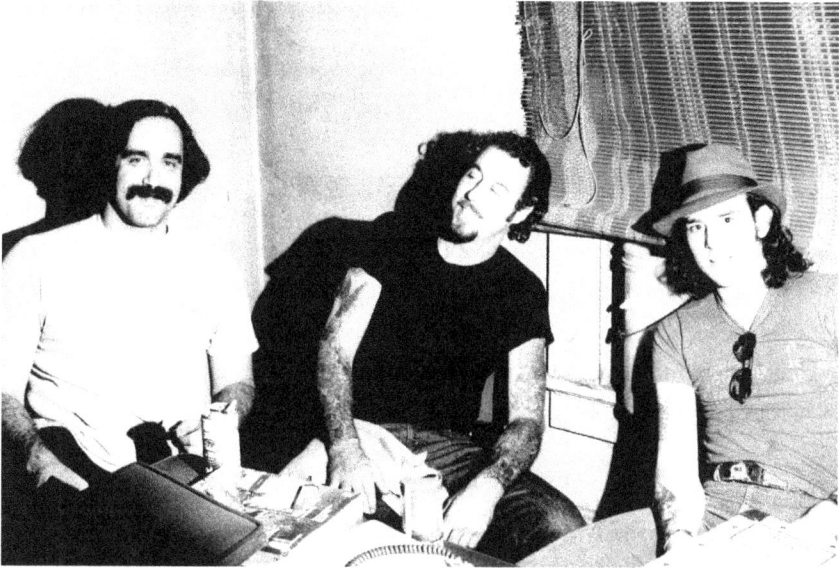

NICK KARRES UPSTAIRS WITH MARK WENNER AND JIMMY THACKERY
OF THE NIGHTHAWKS, 1978.
Photo by Pat Shanklin/Double Door archives

DOUBLE DOOR INN SOFTBALL TEAM WITH THEIR TOURNAMENT TROPHY,
1975. Standing left to right, Doug McRae, Nick Karres, Dennis Martin, Tom Tate, Mike Payne,
Terch Whitesides, Cam McRae. Kneeling left to right, Mike Cassel, Jim Morris, Lenny Federal.
Courtesy Double Door Inn archives

"The reputation of this business was built by providing good music, good service and cold beer," adds Martin. "Many of those who come in have the feeling of being at home, sort of like a neighborhood pub."

Woody Mitchell, a local writer and musician, was among those early Double Door patrons. "In the early going, the Double Door was the neighborhood hangout for the area of the Elizabeth neighborhood around the now defunct Stanley's Drug Store, where countercultural types could get all the necessities of life. Rent in the area was absurdly cheap then and a lot of musicians, artists, and other assorted oddballs shared the old houses and apartments, forming a loose community that naturally gravitated to what we called the bar.

"People started bringing their acoustic guitars in and sitting around on barstools singing songs everybody knew or ones they had just written. The late Jon Mullis was the ringleader, and I recall Michael Brett, Jack Lawrence, Davey Long and Jim Nicholson chiming in at various times, plus a dozen others I can't remember at the moment."

According to the Karres brothers, "the first live music was performed in what is now the game room. One of their friends, Tim Beaver, installed red and black carpet and those who wanted to listen to the music paid 25 or 50 cents to be admitted to the area and sit on the floor. The first musician who performed was Wayne Erbsen, a guitar and banjo player. He was followed by many eager local musicians including Jon Mullis, Michael Brett, Lenny Federal and others too numerous to mention. The success of this early attempt to provide an inviting atmosphere where one could relax with friends, hang out, and actually listen to live music is probably one of the cornerstones of what became the Charlotte live music scene."

"At some point it dawned on Nick that he could draw a crowd if he actually staged musical events," adds Woody Mitchell. "It was all acoustic at first, and being an electric guitar guy, I didn't play there much except to sit in on acoustic occasionally with Jon or whomever. In 1974, John Wicker and I cranked up a band called Paradox, playing a rockin' blend of the esoteric and the nutty. Somehow, we talked Nick into trying electric music and it went over well. To my knowledge, we were the first electric band to play the Double Door.

DOUBLE DOOR TAVERN

a college atmosphere you have been waiting for..
·o· featuring ·o·
every sunday night: wayne erbsen,
mon & wed: john mullis, bret, lenny federal, mike styers
tuesday: chicken cannonball. and dave long

cold beer — imported, draft
sandwiches, games

across from CPCC
next to carolina water bed

ORIGINAL DOUBLE DOOR INN AD, CIRCA 1974.
Courtesy Double Door Inn archives

"By the next year, Lenny Federal and I had joined forces in the Renegade Blues Band. We played Lenny's spirited folk-rock, my raunchy blues-based stuff, and this new music roaring out of Jamaica, reggae. By this time, the Double Door was bringing in local bands every weekend for a two-night stand, with Davey Long doing the booking. There wasn't an actual stage. They'd clear out the area where the stage is now and we'd set up on the floor against the front wall."

Although his bands and accompanying players changed over the years, Lenny Federal has kept on playing. As Woody Mitchell mentioned earlier, he and Lenny formed the Renegade Blues Band quite early in the history of the venue. Some of the other names that his bands claimed were Lenny Don't Surf, The Buddy-Ro Band, The Federal Brothers and the almost infamous Federal Bureau of Rock & Roll. The FBR&R, as they were often referred to, played many Sunday nights as the house band. It was quite a well-known event. Not much was open on a Sunday night and many of the regulars at these shows referred to it as going to Sunday services.

There were many different musicians who played with Lenny, a guitar virtuoso as well as a self described "guitar-wrestler." Some of those included Jack Lawrence (who later played with Doc Watson), Bill Walpole (a prolific songwriter that is still active today), Wendell Elliott, Mahlon Thomas, brother Michael Federal, and others too numerous to recount. Lenny always had the reputation as being very supportive of the music scene and spent many evenings sharing his talents with the crowd at the bar. Davey Long describes Lenny this way. "Lenny set the standard for musicians who followed. He is an absolutely remarkable guitar player and I feel that he is just as good as almost anyone who has ever graced the Double Door stage."

Rob Thorne, longtime drummer of the Spongetones, recalls the atmosphere that surrounded the Double Door during that time. "The first time I went to the Double Door, it was just a beer joint. Just a bar, a local watering hole. Then they started having live acoustic music with Jon Mullis and other players. The live music at the venue was strictly acoustic. Davey Long often played with Mullis as well. All of the players at that point in time had come out of the folk music scene and the Double Door was a perfect place for them to play to live audiences."

LENNY FEDERAL, HALLOWEEN 1975.
Photo by Debbie Shott.

SHEILA CARLISLE OF ARHOOLY, LATE 1970s.
Courtesy Double Door Inn archives

"Nick wasn't letting grass grow under his feet, though," adds Mitchell. "He decided to take the plunge and hire a name from out of town, hoping people would pay a (gasp!) cover charge to hear good entertainment. Davey booked Larry Jon Wilson, who was known as one of the outlaw country music singer/songwriters, and hailed from Augusta, Georgia. To everyone's delight and relief, listeners showed up in droves. Jon Mullis opened the show, with Karen Deane on vocals and me on acoustic lead. Larry Jon won the crowd over and got a great response. For the final tune of the night, he got Jon, Karen and me up to sing harmonies on 'Geronimo's Cadillac.' A real Kodak moment." The event's success became a launching pad for an even bigger show soon afterwards.

According to Nick Karres, "Our real breakthrough came when we had an opportunity to book a nationally known band, the Dixie Dregs for a show. By this time, we had moved the music to the front corner of the building but we didn't have a stage. For a nationally known band, we felt that the least we could do was build a stage."

The opportunity to hire this band came about due to a peculiar set of circumstances. Davey Long recounts it this way. "Steve Nichols was driving to work at Reliable Music, and he sees these two hippies hitchhiking beside the road. He picks 'em up and they ask, 'We're going to Reliable Music. Do you know where that is?' Steve said, 'I'm going there!' Turns out they were members of the Dregs, looking for an Alembic bass. They'd flown in on [Dixie Dregs lead guitarist] Steve Morse's private plane and hitchhiked from the airport. The guys asked Steve [Nichols] if there's anywhere to play in town, and Steve said sure. The Double Door Inn!"

Davey followed up on this contact and was able to book the Dregs for a show at the Double Door in May of 1976. "Once the Dixie Dregs played here and I heard such a wonderful band live in an intimate setting, I was hooked. The music began to be the most important reason to keep going, at least for me," states Nick Karres.

"I saw the Dixie Dregs there," says Rob Thorne. "By that time, no other bar was doing what the Karres brothers were doing. There was no other place to play in Charlotte. Every other bar in town was hiring cover bands that played top forty hits or else they were strictly into country or R&B. Initially, it was pretty loosely organized. You could just sit in with people and play. It was good for an audience.

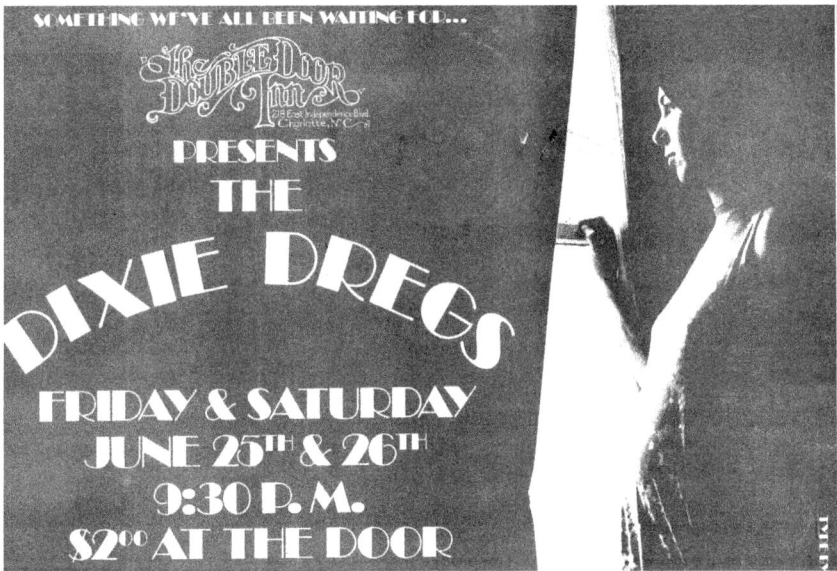

DIXIE DREGS SHOW FLYER, 1976.
Courtesy Double Door Inn archives

They always knew they were going to hear some good live music.

"The Dregs often played with the Nighthawks from Washington, DC, and told them about our venue," adds Nick Karres. "The Nighthawks were immensely popular in the DC area, and they frequently passed through the Charlotte area on their tour to play in places like Atlanta, but previously had found no place to play anywhere near this location. They called us after being referred by members of the Dixie Dregs. We hired them for a show, and their blues and southern rock sound went over quite well."

In April 2008, I was able to speak with Mark Wenner, one of the founding members of the Nighthawks. Wenner stated that the original Nighthawks band formed in the spring of 1972 in the DC area. They played frequently with the Dixie Dregs and had opened for several legendary blues acts, including Muddy Waters. At that time, there were two main circuits that traveling bands followed in order to get the most gigs as possible along the way. The Nighthawks generally traveled from somewhere around Boston to Atlanta, stopping for gigs along the way. After playing to a good response at the Double Door, Charlotte became a main stop on their tours. Wenner shared, "I've known Nick for over 30 years and he is just a great guy. Every time we come through, we usually talk about maybe finally hanging it up and doing something else but the Double Door is still hanging in there and so am I. Nick has always been kind, considerate and honest in all of his dealings with my band."

Nick became acquainted with the band members and they supplied him with a list of other traveling bands that passed through the area and encouraged him to try and hire some of these bands to play at the Double Door. Most of the bands on the list played some form of blues music, and this was probably one of the reasons that the Double Door became a well-known venue for those who were fans of blues music. Some of the bands on that list were Roomfull of Blues, The Fabulous Thunderbirds, Catfish Hodge, and Skip Castro. Another name on that list was Robert Lockwood Jr. (or Robert Jr. Lockwood, as he was sometimes billed), who had learned to play the guitar with the help of his onetime stepfather, Robert Johnson.

The live music scene that originated out of the circumstances and the Karres brothers ability to provide a comfortable, inviting, safe place for the growing

MARK WENNER OF THE NIGHTHAWKS POINTING TO HIS BAND'S NAME ON THE GREEN ROOM WALL, APRIL 2008. Photo by Daniel Coston.

STAGE AREA OF DOUBLE DOOR INN, CIRCA LATE 1970s. Courtesy Double Door Inn archives crowds of music fans is most certainly one of the main reasons for the venue's longevity. Their ability to provide a quality live music experience as well as the ability to attract a wider audience as the business grew has certainly contributed to its success.

By the late 1970s, the Double Door Inn and its tradition as both a neighborhood hangout as well as a well-respected blues venue had led to many nights of incredible music, camaraderie, an occasional drunk or two but all in all, most things were going pretty well for the business. Many local bands were starting to coalesce, play gigs around the area including the Double Door, and more and more of the truly elite musicians from all over were stopping by the Double Door and drawing capacity crowds. There were many nights when it was quite literally shoulder to shoulder, bodies packed together in the old house and always the music ringing out above the din.

"The crowds were crazy," recalls Woody Mitchell. "Everybody came early and stayed late. By this time, Nick had put in an actual stage, but the bar hadn't been pushed back to extend the room yet. Everybody was crammed into the space between the big columns and the west wall. Looking toward the back of the room from the stage, through a turgid cloud of tobacco smoke as thick as a London fog, all you could see was people, occupying every square inch of space. George (Mandrapillias) and Martino (Mike Martin) were whirling dervishes behind the bar, slinging beers out as fast as people could pay for them. No liquor then, it was still against the law to sell it in a club."

More nationally known acts were playing at the Double Door more and more frequently. Most of the music could be classified as blues music, but there were other memorable evenings with bands that also brought in the crowds. Some of the nationally known bands that were starting to play gigs included the Turtles, and Sam and Dave, the famous R&B duo. Despite touring without original singer Sam Moore, they put on quite a show, filling the stage with a full band, including a horn section. The Nighthawks continued to play regularly, as well as their friends the Fabulous Thunderbirds. Many times, these and other bands were booked for Friday and Saturday nights and packed the place on both nights.

The music scene during this period of time should also be considered when evaluating just how much history has been made in the old house that is home

SAM & DAVE, 1978.
Courtesy Double Door Inn archives

to both musicians and fans. The fact that the Double Door began to become well known enough to attract nationally known blues acts such as the Nighthawks, the Fabulous Thunderbirds and others is significant to anyone who is a true fan of the blues.

On the whole, blues music like other genres of music, went through periods of vibrant growth and popularity followed by times when the music lost some of its allure. Music played on the radio was the first music that introduced a whole generation to different styles of music that were evolving in the popular culture of the time. The 1960s brought the British invasion of bands like the Beatles, The Rolling Stones, the Dave Clark Five and others. Jake Berger, a longtime Charlotte musician, observes, "By the time the Double Door opened, most people were listening to what they could hear on the radio. Some of the great soul music greats had passed on, and the blues was definitely in a decline. No one listened to that music at all. I believe that it was guys like Nick who helped Blues music survive until it got healthy again."

Mac Arnold, a left-handed bass player who hails from Greenville, South Carolina, played with the Muddy Waters Blues band from 1966 to 1967. "I remember those old days. I was still a young man but I traveled with the band all over the country. Muddy had two black Cadillacs and that was the way we got from gig to gig. It was quite difficult as it cost money to travel and most of our gigs did not pay that much." Arnold met Waters in Chicago where he had moved to pursue his dream of playing music for a living. Blues music managed to survive in the blues clubs located on the South Side of Chicago but by 1973, blues music had quietly retreated from the spotlight in most of the country.

A young man in Chicago by the name of Bruce Iglauer was a real blues fanatic. He started a blues record company, Alligator Records in Chicago. He distributed his recordings the old-fashioned way by literally selling records out of the trunk of his car. In 1971, Iglauer recorded an album by Hound Dog Taylor and his band the Houserockers using his own money. The album was the first release on the Alligator label. Iglauer began to look for more talent but by 1977, the fledgling label had only released nine albums. In 1978, things began to look up for the small company. Alligator Records released an album entitled Ice Pickin' by a veteran blues guitarist, Albert Collins. This album was nominated for a Grammy and this was just what was needed to help Alligator move to the next level. 1978 marked

JAKE BERGER MAKES A POINT IN THE
DRESSING ROOM, 1999. Photo by Daniel Coston

CALVIN "SANTA CLAUS" JACKSON AND
NICK KARRES, FIFTH ANNIVERSERY
PARTY, DECEMBER 1978.
Photo by Pat Shanklin/Double Door archives

a turning point for the company, as the label received a total of four Grammy nominations that year.

Of course, there were other small, independent labels releasing blues records in the seventies and early eighties. Some of the major record companies occasionally released some Blues or blues influenced music. Warner Brothers issued records made by Texas boogie band ZZ Top as well as records by the multitalented Bonnie Raitt. Even though the business of blues music continued to suffer up until the mid-1980s, there were still many places where traveling blues musicians were welcomed and appreciated. One such place was the Double Door Inn.

After the Nighthawks had first played at the Double Door in the mid-seventies, the club was able to book The Fabulous Thunderbirds out of Austin, Texas for several shows over several years. Guitarist Jimmie Vaughn and singer-harmonica player Kim Wilson led the band that was one of the first blues-based bands to come out of the Austin blues scene. The Thunderbirds formed in 1974 but did not release an album until 1979. The real breakthrough for this band came in 1986 with the release of the song "Tuff Enuff." This song made it into the Top Ten of the Billboard pop charts.

But it was Jimmie Vaughn's younger brother who would go on to revitalize the national blues scene. His name, of course, was Stevie Ray Vaughn. In 1972, he joined a band known as the Nightcrawlers. Later, he formed a blues-rock group with singer Lou Ann Barton that went by the name Triple Threat Revue. In 1978, after the departure of Barton from the group, Vaughn formed his famous band Double Trouble. This is the band that first played at the Double Door in 1979.

More and more alliances were beginning to build among regular patrons and there was often a party atmosphere in the parking lot after the shows. Mookie Brill, a talented bass player and winner of two Blues Music Awards (the Grammys of the blues world), remembers being a young guy who attended many of the shows, and was fortunate enough to often hang out for awhile after the show. "We would just sit out on the cars and shoot the shit," he remembers. Sometimes these impromptu gatherings would last late into the night.

"The first time I saw Stevie Ray Vaughn was there, and it was in October, 1979," Brill adds. "The band was called Double Trouble and they were scheduled for a

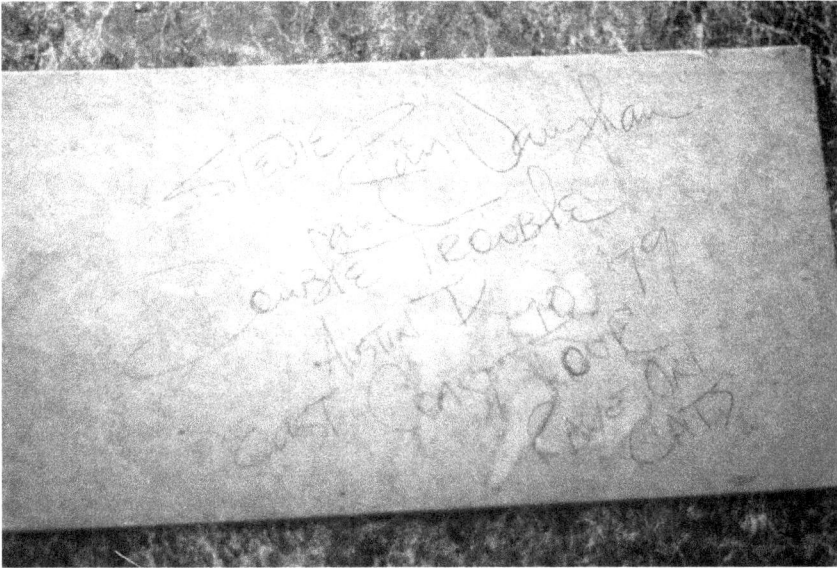

STEVIE RAY VAUGHN'S SIGNATURE, FOUND WEDGED BEHIND A MIRROR IN THE CLUB'S ORIGINAL RESTROOM. Photo by Daniel Coston

DOUBLE DOOR INN BAR, LATE 1970s.
Courtesy Double Door Inn archives

two-day weekend. I went in there and I was just knocked out by Stevie. I thought 'this guy's going to be huge one day'. In fact, when they were knocking out the old bathrooms, there was a towel rack and someone had broken the mirror and on the cardboard underneath, Stevie Ray had signed his autograph. At the time, no one knew how big he was going to be some day so I took it. In fact, I still have it. It's a completely different signature than the one he used later on."

Another musician who shares some of these parking lot memories is Scott Cable. According to Cable, "Touring bands would come through, and be so cool and accessible. They were happy to have whatever crowd came and after gigs, Mookie, myself, and others would often hang with bands in the parking lot. We often listened to cassettes of whatever we had. Big Walter, Magic Sam, The Fabulous Thunderbirds, Chicago Bob Nelson, Eddie Shaw and others. The Legendary Blues Band with Pinetop Perkins were all open and friendly, just talking and drinking beer with us. At the age of seventeen, these guys were like huge stars to me and some of them could not always afford hotel rooms. Often bands would crash at my house to save money. My mom and dad would wake up to sometimes find six or seven guys passed out in the living room. The Double Door opened a lot of doors for us."

When asked how he felt about Nick and the Double Door, Brill replied, "Nick IS the Double Door. I started going there in 1977 and I would often have my coffee with Nick. And I remember that even though I was young, he respected my opinions and would ask what I thought about various things. That was big to me at the time."

"I was also there when [legendary blues musician and songwriter] Willie Dixon played," Brill continues. "At that time he was still bringing the bass fiddle out. He would do three or four songs on the fiddle and then he would sing. His sons were in the band along with Carey Bell, and Chico Chism on the drums." Brill has traveled around the world playing music but when asked how it felt to come back and play on the stage in the Double Door, "It's like going back in the living room!" he says. "I used to live around the corner from there for more than ten years, so it was sort of like my living room. In fact, Nick was the one who gave me the name Mookie. He thought I looked like Ed 'Kookie' Burns on Sunset Strip."

MOOKIE BRILL WITH NAPPY BROWN, DECEMBER 2006.
Photo by Daniel Coston

Scott Cable, a musician who has played several different roles in the ever evolving Charlotte live music scene, shares the following story. "The Double Door Inn is where I first met Carey Bell. Who knew I would end up being his band leader some fifteen years later? I was always the youngster in the crowd. I grew a goatee to try and look older, but it didn't really work. I was not a very good guitar player back then. Mookie [Brill] had been playing awhile by the time I started hanging around, but bands were gracious and let me sit in even though I was pretty bad. I remember Jo Dawkins introducing me to Stevie Ray Vaughn in the dressing room. She said 'Scott, this is the incredible Stevie Vaughn.' Stevie kind of looked at the floor and said, 'Aww, I ain't that good.' We hung for awhile and talked. He was a real nice guy. They later stole some trays or something from the hotel, and Jo called me the next day to see if they could stay at my place as they couldn't afford a room for the night. Stevie later told me that they had not been paid for the Bowie record yet!" Vaughn and Double Trouble would go on to play the Double Door three times between 1979 and 1982.

While many bars would gladly boast those early Vaughn shows as their finest moment, the Double Door's most famous show would fall into Nick Karres' lap just a few years later. "In 1982, I received a phone call from an executive in New York who told me that we were going to have someone unexpected come into our business in about a month. I had no idea who he was talking about but later, I was driving home and I heard a radio ad for an upcoming Eric Clapton show at the old "chrome dome" coliseum. That was about the same time that we had the Legendary Blues Band scheduled for a show. Back then, that band consisted of many former members of the Muddy Waters Band and they had played with Clapton previously. Jerry Portnoy was also in the band and when I heard the commercial, I felt chills go over my body. The Legendary Blues Band was scheduled for a Monday night show. We told a few people that they might want to drop by but Clapton did not show. One of the most unusual things that happened was that we already had local musician Bill Noonan scheduled for that Thursday night, and Legendary Blues band had a scheduled gig in Atlanta. Their gig was canceled and they decided to spend a few days in Charlotte. This was one of the key events that made everything work.

Clapton was basing his tour out of Charlotte at the same time. He and his managers and entourage were staying at the Radisson Hotel. Portnoy was talking to Clapton during this time and hoping to make something happen. Clapton

CAREY BELL, 2005.
Photo by Daniel Coston

played the Charlotte Coliseum on Wednesday night, June 23 but he did not come in that night. Many people still believe that this is the night he played at the Double Door after that show, but it did not happen that way. He actually came in on Thursday night, June 24, 1982 after playing a show in Tennessee and flying back to Charlotte. Clapton and Portnoy agreed that he would sit in with the Legendary Blues Band that night at the Double Door. Then Legendary Blues Band requested to play that night and we quickly called Bill Noonan who agreed to do a very short set so that we could accommodate Portnoy's request. In fact, Noonan still tells people that [he] got bumped for Clapton. We were never really certain if this appearance would really happen but we wanted to accommodate such a blues legend if at all possible."

Clapton came into the Double sometime around midnight, and watched the band play for more than an hour. Karres estimated that there were about 30 to 35 people in attendance but that after Clapton showed up, there was a long line at the pay phone in the front where people called everyone they knew and told them to come for the show.

By the time the Legendary Blues Band asked him to come and sit in with the band, there were maybe about ninety people actually present. Clapton walked to the stage and plugged in a worn Stratocaster guitar. He played five songs with the band and then one encore. However, he did not sing. After the show, he did hang around with Portnoy and the band in their dressing room, by then known as the bar's "Green Room." While in the dressing room, someone was mindful enough to snap a picture of Clapton with the band, and this photo remains the best-known picture ever taken at the Double Door.

Even years after this extraordinary event occurred, whenever Clapton visits Charlotte, rumors abound that he might once more stroll into the Double Door Inn. In the intervening years, the people who "say" that they were there that night has grown well beyond those actual 90 people. Among the many items behind the bar is a t-shirt that was made for one of the Double Door's many anniversaries. The back of it reads, "I was there when Eric played! Yeah, right!"

Another musician who played at the Door, as it was often referred to by this point, was an outrageous fellow known as Root Boy Slim. He was acquainted with the Nighthawks Band and that is one of the connections that landed him a spot on

ERIC CLAPTON WITH THE LEGENDARY BLUES BAND UPSTAIRS IN
THE DRESSING ROOM, MARCH 1982. Jerry Portnoy, seated in center, directly
behind Clapton, Pinetop Perkins seated next to Portnoy on his left.
Courtesy Double Door Inn archives

PINETOP PERKINS, MAY 2004.
Photo by Daniel Coston

IN WITNESS WHEREOF, the parties hereto have hereunto set their names and seals on the day and year first above written.

NICK KARRES			WILLIE DIXON		10-208
Print Purchaser's Full and Correct Name (If Purchaser is Corporation, Full and Correct Corporate Name)			Print Name of Signatory Musician		Home Local Union No.
X _Fred Karns_			X _Willie Dixon By Mary_		
Signature of Purchaser (or Agent thereof)			Signature of Signatory Musician		
Double Door, 218 E. Independence Blvd.			c/o Cameron, 2700 Cahuenga East 4103		
Street Address			Musician's Home Address		
Charlotte, NC 28204			Los Angeles, CA 90068		
City	State	Zip Code	City	State	Zip Code
704-372-3057 club			415-386-3456		
Telephone			Telephone		
Mike Kappus		9736	P.O. Box 210103 San Francisco, CA 94121		
Booking Agent		Agreement No.	Address		

WILLIE DIXON'S CONTRACT FOR HIS APPEARANCE IN 1984.
Courtesy Double Door Inn archives

JUNIOR WALKER, 1984.
Courtesy Double Door Inn archives

the calendar. His real name was Foster McKenzie III. His father was a golf course architect, and their family lived in the nation's capital.

McKenzie attended several prestigious private schools and eventually ended up studying at Yale University, a bastion of the Ivy League. Root Boy, as he came to be known, made the acquaintance of a bass player named Bob Greenlee. Greenlee was also captain of the Yale football team and a fraternity brother. The two kindred spirits formed a band known as Prince La-la Percy, Percy Uptight and the Midnight Creepers. Their most notable accomplishment was never playing the same venue twice.

Root Boy and Greenlee went on the road to play outrageous shows. Slim was a large man and he became known as "300 pounds of dynamite with a two-inch fuse." His band took on the name Root Boy Slim and the Sexchange Band. The band knew how to use shock lyrics and antics to draw the audience in. Slim often came on stage wearing a straitjacket and mumbled half sentences and made often bizarre statements that made sense only to him. Sadly, Slim passed away in Florida in 1993. There is still a framed poster that reads "Root Boy Slim & the Sexchange Band" mounted on the wall behind the bar at the Double Door Inn.

According to the International Blues Foundation, located in Memphis, Tennessee, there is not a blues venue anywhere around that has continued to operate under the same management, in the same location for this period of time. The Charlotte Observer also credits the establishment as being the oldest live music venue located in the same building with the same ownership and management in the country. There has been some debate about this however, so the Double Door considers itself the second oldest blues bar in the country.

Regardless, 35 years in the same place doing the same thing with the same ownership and management is very rare. That is quite a reputation to uphold and the fact that it is often referred to as "The World Famous Double Door Inn" is well deserved. The question remains, why this place? Why these owners? Of all the honky-tonks and juke joints and other music venues that exist, what makes this old, run down house, originally built in 1911, have such staying power, appeal and great reputation among fans and musicians alike?

DOUBLE DOOR INN EXTERIOR, 1981.
Courtesy Double Door Inn archives

Looking back, the answer must lie somewhere in the ownership and management practices over a long 35 year history in the community. Before they inadvertently fell into the business of being in charge of such a place, neither of the Karres brothers had any idea that their idea of opening a small bar where young people could go to hang out would turn into such a well-known music venue that would draw world-class performers to it s intimate stage. After the music began to be more of a focus for the business, Nick Karres wanted to provide great music as often as possible to his patrons. "I felt that if we could offer really quality music, we would be different from just another bar," he stated.

Karres went on to add, "Back then, we were what was known as a "groundbreaker" club. Being a groundbreaking club, we often hired bands that no one knew. That is, they were not always commercial successes and they weren't heard on the radio, but we took our chances. We sometimes really stuck our neck out, and sometimes we lost money. I feel that one of the best things we have done was to take many chances trying to do the right thing by providing great music. But we were definitely not driven by the bottom line. That is also part of the reputation and legacy of the Double Door. It has always been a risky venture. For example, the first time Stevie Ray Vaughn played here, we only had six people in the audience and that included the bartender. The second time he played here, we drew about thirty people and by the third (and last) time he played here, we had maybe about a hundred people turn out.

Once you take so many chances over the years, it gives you a feeling I can't really describe. A serious businessperson would have never done business this way. If money had been my biggest motivator, I would have run a hotel bar and brought in top forty bands. However to me, the most important thing that we have accomplished over the years is the fact that we are still here. I've always felt that one should always try to do the best he can with what he has, and that is what we have strived to do here. What I am proud of is what we have accomplished. This building was not built to be a music venue, it was someone's residence at one time."

"I always have gotten my satisfaction from setting up great shows," adds Karres. "I don t have to be in the forefront of announcing from the stage. My satisfaction comes from making shows that feature great musicians possible. Unfortunately, it is hard to predict whether the business will make money on any one particular

MATTHEW AND NICK KARRES, DOUBLE DOOR INN 10TH
ANNIVERSARY SHOW, 1983. Courtesy Double Door Inn archives

show. So it really has to be a labor of love to run a venue such as this one on such a small scale."

Looking back over the many years that the Double Door has survived as a blues music venue as well as introducing other genres of music to the live music scene, it is easy to see a pattern that is much like blues music itself. Both the music and the business have had their share of ups and downs, but both continue to endure. Along with promoting blues music, many may not be aware that reggae music was first played live in Charlotte at the Double Door Inn. The band was Awareness Arts Ensemble. Their music was well received as was the zydeco music that was played early on by bands such as Nathan and the Zydeco Cha-Chas, and future Grammy winner Terence Simien and his zydeco band.

Another musician who has continued to play frequently at the Double Door since the fall of 1979 is Bob Margolin. Margolin played in the Muddy Waters Blues Band during the years 1973-1980. "By late 1979 I could see that I would soon be starting my own band and during a time when Muddy was off, a friend of mine who lived in Washington, DC but was from North Carolina booked some NC dates for me. One of them was the Double Door in the Fall of 1979," Margolin says.

"The Double Door was a very typical music club and I've always enjoyed playing there. I think it's significant that The Double Door has provided thousands of nights of good entertainment for its neighbors", adds Margolin. "A lot of good times were had in that building. I'm sure that over the last 29 years I've played there dozens of times. I'm very at home on that bandstand. In a world that has gone to increasingly big-time corporate-marketed entertainment, the Double Door brings its bands and audiences together in a way that's real, in-the-moment, and ultimately more satisfying than watching TV, a computer, or seeing an elaborately staged arena show. The audience and the performers can meet and become friends. I know that running a live music club can be an opportunity to lose a lot of money and it's a tribute to Nick's strength and persistence that he s been able to keep the place going."

Even before the Double Door officially opened its doors, it had already caught the interest of several young musicians in the area. One of these who went on to play music in a variety of different bands is Jake Berger. "I went in there about a week

BOB MARGOLIN, LATE 1970s.
Courtesy Double Door Inn archives

before the place really opened and had a beer and talked to Nick," says Berger. "So I remember that before they started having live music, the bar was quite small. Where the kitchen is now was then the game room. You could walk in, walk around, go upstairs and when you came down you would be in the game room. It was weird. It was just an old house. When they first started having acoustic music, it was located in the back room that is now the game room. Lenny Federal was one of the first acoustic guitarists that I saw play there. There was no sound equipment and there was just a corner for the band to stand and play for the audience that was often seated on the floor. I remember the band that Lenny and Woody had called the Renegade Blues Band. They played the first reggae song that I ever heard and they were quite good."

Berger had his own odyssey throughout the 1970s and 1980s, as he played with many bands and even traveled away from his Charlotte base to follow his musical muse. Rob Thorne of the Spongetones notes, "Jake Berger has put together more bands in town than anyone I know."

That includes the Spongetones themselves, who have since gone on to record eleven albums, and continue to have a devoted fanbase around the world. Founded in 1978 by Berger, Thorne, guitarist Pat Walters, bassist Steve Stoeckel, and drummer, their collective love of British Invasion-influenced 1960s rock formed the basis of their sound.

The Spongetones played their first live gig at another local bar, the Hitchin' Post. Immediately after this show, Jake Berger bowed out from the Spongetones and Keith Brooks briefly joined the band. He was then replaced when Jamie Hoover joined the band in 1980. By 1982, their first album, Beat Music, was garnering rave reviews in Rolling Stone Magazine, and bringing in some of the biggest crowds that the Double Door has ever seen.

"I believe the Double Door is the second place we ever played," Thorne adds. "It gave us a chance to formulate what we were all about and people just ate it up. We, the Spongetones, have played some of our best shows at the Double Door. The crowd that used to come out to see us play has changed. Now, their kids come out to see us. For over 30 years, it's been the best place to play. I hope it lasts forever."

SPONGETONES POSTER, 1982.
Courtesy Double Door Inn archives

"We saw a lot of clubs and club owners come and go," continues Thorne. "But with the Double Door, we trusted them completely, and that's rare. Nick Karres is an anomaly in the business. We always tried to be respectful of the club and their patrons and we 'have always gotten that back. It s always great to see people mix so well. It s relaxed and you know the people at the bar want you there."

"The Spongetones were, and to a lot of people, still are massively huge," says Daniel Coston, a longtime documentarian of the Charlotte music scene. "They were one of the first local bands that made their Double Door shows an event. All of these years later, their shows are still something to see. They were one of the acts that redefined what Charlotte musicians could do on a national, or even international scale."

During the late 1970s and into the early 1980s, the Karres brothers continued doing business and attracting more attention as they were able to book more and more well known blues acts to play music for the crowds that would pack the place for a chance to be a part of the scene. Many people in the Charlotte area have their own favorite Double Door story. There were couples who met and later married each other, as well as those who celebrated birthdays and anniversaries by treating themselves to a night out at the Double Door. The reputation of the business grew and more people decided to drop by to see what their friends were talking about. Of course, there was a little bit of uneasiness felt by some people about going into such a dimly lit place that served alcohol, and even had a "head shop" right next door.

I would meet people," adds Rob Thorne, "and they would say, 'Oh, I've heard about the Double Door, but I'm not sure if I should go.' And I'd say, 'You've got to come. You've just got the experience the Double Door.' We've brought a lot of people that otherwise would've never gone there. But once they do it, they always said, 'What a great place.' They think it's just great."

In June of 2008, I was able to speak with another musician who played shows at the Double Door Inn. His name is Bill Blue and his band was known as The Bill Blue Band. Blue resided in Key West, Florida for more than 20 years but now builds dobros in his small guitar shop in New Smyrna Beach, Florida. He still occasionally plays music and does tours in the Florida area.

SPONGETONES, CD RELEASE PARTY FOR THEIR 11TH ALBUM,
TOO CLEVER BY HALF, MAY 2008. Photo by Daniel Coston.

When Blue was a younger musician, he told me that "the Double Door was known among many musicians I knew as the place to play. Blue greatly admired the band the Nighthawks, and asked his agent to try and book him everywhere that the Nighthawks had played. "That was how I first came to play at the Double Door," he says. From the years from 1978 to 1984, Blue stated that the Double Door was considered one of the premier places for Blues musicians to play in the South. "I remember the very first time that my band played there. I was upstairs with my guys and I remember telling them that I wanted everyone to play really, really well. I definitely came of age in the music business during this time. We always had great gigs and Nick and Matt always treated us very well each time we came to town. It was one of our all-time favorite places to play. One thing that really made this venue special was that people actually came out to listen to the music."

Up until about 1980 or so, there was a small building located where the front part of the parking area is now located, with the unforgettable title of Chronosynclasticinfidibulum. Originally, the building had been a Toddle House Restaurant. Toddle House, was a restaurant that served breakfast and was open 24 hours daily, seven days a week. This building had been converted to what was known among the hippie countercultural types as a head shop. "Head shops," for those who may not be aware, generally cater to people who are looking for alternative merchandise such as pipes, rolling papers and other supplies necessary for those who partake of marijuana. Sometime around late 1980 or 1981, the building burned, and was demolished in order to ease access to the small parking lot beside the Double Door.

As the years went by, the two brothers continued to work together doing all of the work behind the scenes that must be attended to in order for a business to survive. They rotated shifts. Some evenings, Matthew would be on duty and Nick would work during the day. Depending on their own personal schedules, they rotated working hours so that both of them were able to keep the business going. Both George Mandripillias and Mike Martin became quite skilled at tending bar, preventing fights and generally just making sure that everything ran as it should. "Many times I've seen George or Mike come over the bar to break up a fight," says Rob Thorne.

Sometime around 1985, Matthew Karres made the decision to move on from the bar business, and left to pursue other interests. As of this writing, Mike "Martino"

CHRONOSYNCLASTICINFINDIBULUM, ORIGINAL BUILDING
NEXT DOOR TO THE DOUBLE DOOR INN, MID 1970s.
Courtesy Double Door Inn archives

GEORGE MANDRAPILLIAS TENDING BAR, EARLY 2008.
Photo by Daniel Coston

Martin still works behind the bar only now, he also mixes drinks as well as slinging beers. After the North Carolina legislature made it legal for some establishments to sell what is known as "liquor by the drink," the Double Door obtained the proper license to sell both wine and liquor.

Most of the employees at the Double Door have worked there for long periods of time. J. Todd Smith has worked there since 1985. He was gracious enough to share the following piece that gives his own perspective of working at the Double Door Inn.

"On my time working at the DDI one would think that the best part would be hearing all of the great music that has been there throughout the years, or meeting the musicians that played there or who just happened to venture in. Another would be meeting all the pro and amateur athletes that have come in. Whether football players, basketball, baseball, golf or NASCAR, they have all been in not to mention all of the local and national media that covered them. Meeting actors and actresses who played in movies that were shot at the DDI. Also politicians of all kinds have been through these doors. Also there have been all sorts of opportunities that have come from working at the DDI such as going to sporting events of all kinds, and I mean in first class, or getting to play golf at historic and exclusively private courses. Or getting backstage passes to huge concerts due to dealing with booking agents. Or all the people I have met along the way, I have made a lot of friends that I hope I will have for the rest of my life."

As Smith mentioned, several movies have been shot at the Double Door, including "Shallow Hal" in 2000, when the bar was dressed up to look like a ski lodge. Some other notable folks that have stopped in to hang out at the bar over the years range from members of the legendary rock band AC/DC, to Dallas Mavericks owner Mark Cuban.

"I can't say that all has been great, but for me it has always been about the laughs. When I was first hired, I also worked with Nick in the afternoons and met many of his childhood friends and heard all of their stories. I heard stories about Nick from high school, college and the early days of the DDI. If it's true that laughter adds years to one's life, then I should live a couple of hundred years. The one constant is working with the staff, those still here but ones who have moved on, and the ones who are no longer alive (Michael Reese, Dave Stone and Basil Coston).

WORKERS REMOVE THE ORIGINAL WINDOW ON THE CLUB'S
SECOND FLOOR, EARLY 1980s. Courtesy Double Door Inn archives

But the absolute best thing about working here is working for Nick Karres. Simply put, he is a good man who gives people chances. If it wasn't for Nick, there is no telling where we would all be today and I want to thank him for that."

Woody Mitchell also shared, "By the 1980s, that scene of some of Charlotte's first live music had given way to the blues era that gave the Double Door its claim to fame. Working in road bands most of that time, I stopped in every time I was in town and tried to keep up with folks. In 1992, I moved back to Charlotte for good and played there in numerous weekend warrior bands, including Woody & the Wingnuts and the Stragglers, and staged or played numerous benefits along the way."

Sponsoring benefits for musicians who were struck by some sort of physical illness or other tragedy has always been a custom at the Double Door. Over the years, countless benefits have been sponsored and held at the facility with all proceeds going to benefit musicians in need of medical care or other life necessities. Glancing at some of the old calendars, several benefits sponsored by the Double Door stand out. Benefits held for local musicians such as Bruce Schneider, Michael Federal and Charles Hairston are just a few of the names that leaped off the page. It is well known throughout Charlotte's music community that if space is needed to stage a show to help raise money for anyone in need, Nick Karres will always go out of his way to help in any way possible.

Over the years, there have been many stories of the generosity that is a large part of Nick's outlook on life. In order to prevent any embarrassment , no names will be used but it is well-known that many bad checks have remained uncollected, loans have not been repaid and many outright gifts have been given to some of the less fortunate by both Karres brothers. During an interview conducted with Nick, he expressed his feelings vehemently about such matters. "It has always been important to me personally to try and always do the right thing."

The Double Door continued to bring in a variety of acts throughout the 1980s, continuing into the early '90s. Walking through the club and looking through the photos on the wall reveals the variety of people that have played there. Buddy Guy, Vassar Clements, Jason and the Scorchers, Roy Buchanan, Steve Forbert, Sugar Blue, Wanda Jackson, John Hammond, Clarence "Gatemouth" Brown, Wet Willie, Steve Earle and many others graced the stage, while local acts such as

CLARENCE "GATEMOUTH" BROWN, 1984.
Courtesy Double Door Inn archives

JOHN HAMMOND, 1986.
Courtesy Double Door Inn archives

the Federal Bureau of Rock and Roll held down regular Sunday or Monday shows there.

Any business entity depends on many professional and personal relationships in order to keep things running as smoothly as possible. The Double Door is no exception. It would be impossible to name all of the people who have contributed to the venue's longevity. One class of people that have played a large part in the story over the years are the booking agents, who assist in getting bands "booked" into venues like the Double Door.

Even though Charlotte is certainly not considered an entertainment base, such as New York or Los Angeles, three of the most successful blues booking agents in the business are located in the city. These include Piedmont Talent, Blue Mountain and Intrepid Artists. These three booking agencies represent a large number of blues acts that are still touring.

During the research for this book, I became well-acquainted with Rick Booth. Booth founded his own agency, Intrepid Artists in 1994. In addition to having booked many of his acts for shows at the Double Door, Booth is also a friend of Nick's and has served as technical consultant as I have written this story. According to Booth, "I used to sneak in with a fake ID back in the early 80s to see the Spongetones and Cruis-O-Matic. I was not there to drink, only to see the music. I knew that if I went down there, I would be in for a treat. Back then, you only had to be eighteen to frequent clubs or drink. We all had fake ID's. I assume that things became more difficult when the drinking age changed to twenty-one. It was all harmless good fun."

At that time of course, Booth had no idea that one day he would be a booking agent and do business with the Double Door. Booth first met Nick Karres around 1990 through business as well as attending some shows. According to Booth, "Some of the first bands that I booked there were Jimmy Thackery & the Assassins, followed by Jimmy Thackery & the Drivers, Johnny "Clyde" Copeland, Chubby Carrier and the Bayou Swamp Band. Over the years, I have booked the likes of Son Seals, Walter Trout, Tab Benoit, Tinsley Ellis, Watermelon Slim, Lil Ed & the Blues Imperials and many, many more."

JOHNNY "CLYDE" COPELAND, 1985.
Courtesy Double Door Inn archives

ROY BUCHANAN, 1988. BUCHANAN DIED A WEEK AFTER THIS SHOW.
Courtesy Double Door Inn archives

GLENN PHILLIPS BAND, 1985.
Photo by Rackley/Double Door archives

THE
FABULOUS
THUNDERBIRDS
IN
CONCERT
TUESDAY
JUNE 4TH 1985
THE
DOUBLE DOOR INN
CHARLOTTE, N.C.

FABULOUS THUNDERBIRDS FLYER, 1985.
Courtesy Double Door Inn archives

The Double Door Inn
CHARLOTTE, N.C.
376-1446

OCTOBER 1986

SUNDAY	MONDAY	TUESDAY	WEDNESDAY	THURSDAY	FRIDAY	SATURDAY
Coming in November: 2 · BLUES BUSTERS (TENT.) 7-8 · UPTOWN RHYTHM KINGS w/ MARK WENNER 12 · A.A.E. 21-22 · ROOT BOY SLIM 23 · ELVIN BISHOP 27 · ARHOOLY 28-29 · KILLER WHALES			1 THE SMOKING PHONES CHAPEL HILL, N.C.	2 THE BELVEDERES BLUES SHOW	3 TOM PRINCIPATO BAND	4
5	6	7 Federal Bros	8 DARRYL RHOADES AND THE MIGHTY MEN from GLAD – FROM ATLANTA –	9	10 BOB MARGOLIN W/ SPECIAL GUEST NAPPY BROWN – FRIDAY NIGHT ONLY! –	11
12	13	14 Federal Bros	15 Barrence Whitfield & the SAVAGES · OPENING ACT The BELVEDERES	16 IDOL CHATTER	17 CRUIS O MATIC	18 the MIGHTY Dramelles
19	20 Fed Bros	21 ITAL REGGAE	22 MIGHTY JOE YOUNG CHICAGO BLUES	23 RORY BLOCK FOLK BLUES W/ SCOTT CABLE SANDY BELL	24 the Heartfixers R&B FROM ATLANTA	25
26	27	28 Federal Bros	29 FREEDOM OF EXPRESSION REGGAE · SKA	30 J.J. CALE IN CONCERT	31 HALLOWEEN PARTY FED BROS.	NOV. 1ST EVAN JOHNS & THE H·BOMBS

The Fed Bros

DOUBLE DOOR INN FLYER, OCTOBER 1986.
Courtesy of Lenny Federal

DOUBLE DOOR INN 15TH ANNIVERSARY FLYER, 1988.
Courtesy Double Door Inn archives

DOUBLE DOOR INN 15TH ANNIVERSARY PARTY, DECEMBER 1988.
Courtesy Double Door Inn archives

When asked about how he felt about the venue and Nick, Booth added, "What can I say? I love Nick. He is one of a kind! He has always gone out of his way to take care of me and to take care of the bands and the people I work with. He has always gone the extra mile for me. There are a lot of people in this world that could learn some diplomacy and many other lessons from Nick. I hold him in very high regard. He runs his business in the way that I like to think that I run mine. Honesty, accountability, hard work and doing it for the love of the business. You know, do unto others as you would have them do unto you. I think it is safe to say that Nick follows that rule."

It should be noted that the Double Door Inn stands for different things to different people. Many people frequent the bar for a quick bite of lunch or a drink between classes at CPCC. Many of these customers may never see a live music show at the venue, yet these folks are also part of the history. Lynn Farris, a music writer who also lives in Charlotte, contributed the following about her own experiences visiting the venue.

"I didn't really come to know the Double Door Inn as most people have. True, I've spent plenty of nights at the club partying with friends, checking out bands, but the first time I walked into the place it was early afternoon, after classes at Central Piedmont Community college (CPCC) across the street. My dad and my brother, friends of Nick from the ball field, had suggested I stop by and introduce myself. To this day, I'm still not even sure if either of them, particularly my church going father, ever set foot inside the club.

"Being only eighteen at the time, the hours I'd accrued patronizing nightclubs was limited, but taking a seat at the Double Door's bar for lunch that day, I looked around and knew I was in a cool place. From the start, I was treated like family, and soon I was spending a lot of time at the Double Door, which may very well be the reason I spent five years at a two year college. But putting in your time during the day offered a different perspective. I had my own breakfast special and Nick even cut me a deal on parking after my car was vandalized at a regular CPCC parking lot. Late afternoons I'd stop in to hang out with the Happy Hour regulars because everybody always had a story to tell. Back then, Nick's wife Betty worked the lunch counter with one of his longtime buddies, Basil. Todd, who a lot of folks now know from working the door at night, was the cook. Missy [who worked at the Double Door throughout the 1990s] came in during the afternoons to help

FRIENDS AND BAR HELP OF THE DOUBLE DOOR INN, EARLY 1990s.
Courtesy Double Door Inn archives

BASIL TAKES CARE OF PATRONS, MID 1990s.
Courtesy Double Door Inn archives

with the bookings and also helped longtime bartenders Mike and George when they needed it. And every once in awhile I'd see Kelly or Cole, Nick and Betty's kids. The Double Door Inn played a significant part of my life. And whatever the future may hold for that little old house that now sits in an area engulfed by new development, our memories and the music we've experienced there make it feel like home."

Over the years, even though the Double Door Inn sometimes seems stuck in time, some things have definitely changed. Presently, the inside and the bar have been redone at least three different times. The bar now stretches all the way down the wall. There are some seats from an old auditorium on the other side of the room. The old booths that were originally installed are long gone. The stage is elevated and there is professional sound equipment and PA available. There is also lighting on the stage that can be shifted depending on the mood.

"I first went to the Double Door in 1994, to one of the Sunday night open mic shows," says Daniel Coston. "I hadn't been to too many bars at that point, so the whole experience was quite something. To this day, I think it's the only time that I sat down and watched a show, apart from when I was sitting on the floor taking pictures of the musicians. I finally started going to the bar on a more regular basis in 1996, as I started writing and taking photos for the now-defunct Tangents Magazine. The more I went, the more I got to know the doormen, the bar people, and all of the various regulars. Sooner or later, whether you recognize it or not, you become a regular there. Just another piece of the funky fabric that makes up the place on any given night."

The decade from 1990 to 2000 were years that were mostly good ones, as far as the venue was concerned. It was a time when local and regional bands played regularly and some of the national traveling acts were often booked and played to good crowds. Part Time Blues Band, Big Brick Building, Tab Benoit, Bob Margolin, Bernard Allison, Tinsley Ellis, Kenny Neal, Smokin' Joe Kubek, and Luther Allison also made appearances as well as others too numerous to recount. In 1993, the Double Door Inn celebrated its twentieth anniversary with a show at the Capri Theater in Charlotte. Jimmy Thackery, Tinsley Ellis, Don Dixon and Marti Jones headlined an evening that Nick Karres is still proud of.

DON DIXON AND MARTI JONES BACKSTAGE AT THE DOUBLE DOOR
INN'S 20 ANNIVERSARY SHOW, CAPRI THEATER, DECEMBER 1993.
Courtesy Double Door Inn archives

BERNARD ALLISON PLAYING ON TOP OF THE DOUBLE DOOR BAR, 1997.
Courtesy Double Door Inn archives

Kevin Outlaw, who refers to himself as "the new guy," began working for Karres in March of 1997. He had first visited the business a few years earlier at age 19 when his then-boss brought him in a few times. His employment began in an informal way. By the time he was twenty-one, he began to hang out as a customer and became known to the night bartenders, Mike and George. At some point, there was a need for someone to fill in at the crucial post of doorman and when asked, Outlaw enthusiastically agreed. Later, the job became six nights a week for awhile but then as he found daytime employment, he became a part-time employee again.

Being the first person that a potential customer encounters as they enter the building for a music event, I was curious as to what things he was responsible for, says Outlaw. "Evaluating people as they come in and being able to screen out potential trouble makers is my most important function. Initially, I wanted to work here regardless of whether I was paid. I've just always thought that this was such a cool place."

Of all of the employees that I spoke with, I found Outlaw to be one of the most enthusiastic and appreciative about being employed by the venue. "I have turned people away at the door if I felt that they were too intoxicated or might present some other problem. I know that I am a real smart ass but in this job, I have learned how to keep my cool and try and make sure that each customer leaves without anger or bitterness towards this business. I feel that all of us who work here are extensions of Nick, and that we should keep that in mind when we are on the job."

According to Outlaw, the best thing about his job is the vibe he feels just from entering the building. Whenever I come in this door, I feel a certain vibe in the air, almost like the wood in here has absorbed the ghosts of blues performers who have passed through here over the years. It is a special ambiance that is present for those who are open to it.

Due to scheduling variations, Outlaw did not have an opportunity to even meet his new boss for the first three or four months of his employment. After he got to know Nick, he knew that he had met a special and unique kind of employer. "Nick is a great boss," he observes. "He never yells. Any issues that might arise, he will always discuss them with me. If you ever need anything, he will help you. He is

TODD SMITH THE DOORMAN, JULY 2008.
Photo by Daniel Coston

DOORMAN KEVIN OUTLAW, JUNE 2008.
Photo by Daniel Coston

really great and always understanding. He always has time to talk to me and he is not like any other boss I've ever seen."

One anecdote Outlaw shares goes a long way towards explaining why he finds the venue so appealing. "Before I started working here, I just happened to be here one afternoon. I observed something that really made me realize the significance of a business like this. There was a CEO of a major corporation, dressed in a professional suit, having a beer at the bar. Beside him was a man who drove a garbage truck for a living. In here, over a beer, the two were having a great conversation. Outside of here, the two would have never spoken a word to each other. That image has stayed with me to this day. That is one of the greatest things I see. People of all ages and backgrounds can come here, feel comfortable and all enjoy themselves."

The Double Door Inn is also home to the Charlotte Blues Society. The Society is affiliated with the International Blues Foundation located in Memphis, Tennessee. The purpose of the Foundation is to help preserve Blues music. Each year, a contest is held in Memphis to determine who should be picked as the International Blues champion. There are two categories, band and solo/duo acts. Most of the Blues societies that are affiliates hold their own regional talent contests in order to pick who will represent them at the prestigious yearly contest. Also, the Foundations sponsors the Blues Music Awards each year which is like the Grammy awards of the Blues. Many musicians who have won some of these awards (previously known as the Handy Awards), have played at the Double Door.

The idea of becoming an affiliate of the International Blues Foundation by starting the Charlotte Blues society came from two sources. Three blues musicians, Beth Pollhammer, James Linton and Bill Buck and Nick Karres. As the Double Door was the only club hiring blues musicians in the Charlotte area at the time, Karres had become interested in helping the Blues acts become more popular locally and boost interest in their music. During the first year of the founding of the Charlotte Blues Society, Beth Pollhamer worked with Nick and some other Society members and in 1994, The Double Door was presented a special award for Keeping the Blues Alive from the International Blues Foundation.

SOUND BOARD AND BACK ROOM, 1993.
Courtesy Double Door Inn archives

LENNY FEDERAL MANNING THE SOUNDBOARD, MID 1990s.
Courtesy Double Door Inn archives

One of the most exciting things that the CBS accomplished was sending a band to the national competition that actually won the IBC. Jim Jervis, a former member of the Society shared the story with me. "I received an unsolicited CD by a band out of Atlanta called Delta Moon from their manager, Nancy Lewis Pegel with Brilliant Productions. She was looking to try and get a local gig for the band. I had received plenty of CD's from bands as the vice president of the Blues Society. I remember it clearly. I was headed out of town on vacation and just happened to bring along the CD Delta Moon. I was struck by the grizzly, mud-drenched sound coming out of my CD player. I mean that I was just blown away and I said to my wife, 'you have to hear these guys. They have it!' Gina Leigh's and Tom Gray's vocals intertwined with Mark (Johnson) and Tom's dual slide guitars backed by a powerful rhythm section just grabbed me!

"I called Nancy and told her that I loved this band. This was a first for me. I quickly was able to make a couple of calls and I got them a gig at the Sylvia Theater in York, SC. I had to see them live. They played to about 15 people. The lack of a crowd did not affect them at all. I began to think about our talent contest. I played the CD for a few folks, most of which loved it. I did have another board member that said to me that he didn't think they stood a chance against some of the other people who were going to compete. I told him otherwise and I said, 'I have your winner here.'"

"The group was reluctant," adds Jervis. "I definitely had to push. I told them that based on my knowledge of the other bands competing I felt that they had as good a chance as anyone to win the CBS contest and go on to Memphis and win it all. The competition was stiff that year as it always is. We have a very strong base of fantastic musicians in this area. I had also negotiated a first place prize of 1,000 CD's and some free studio time for the winner. This helped get the band onboard. I also stressed to them that it would help them get a booking at the Double Door which they had not been able to crack before. It did help. They won our contest in Charlotte, went on to win in Memphis and now play several times a year at the Double Door.

Through members' support and co-sponsorships, the society has helped bring many artists to the area for the first time. Some of these include Drink Small, Big Jack Johnson, Lightnin' Wells, Johnny Whitlock and many more. The Blues Sunday meetings are free to members and feature local, regional and national

THE DOUBLE DOOR, 1990s.
Courtesy Double Door Inn archives

GREGG MCGRAW, AMERICANA NIGHT PROMOTER WITH NICK KARRES,
1997. Courtesy Double Door Inn archives

talent along with an Open-Mic Jam. There is also a monthly newsletter printed and each year, contests are held to determine who will represent the Charlotte Blues Society in Memphis.

By 1997, there was an emerging scene of musicians throughout North Carolina that infused rock with country and folk music, a mix that was often tagged with the "Americana" label. The Double Door quickly became home to a collective of Americana acts like the Rank Outsiders, and David Childers. Gregg McCraw, who had been promoting Rank Outsiders shows, also began promoting a "Americana Night" every Tuesday evening, bringing in national acts to play alongside the local groups.

"The Showcase itself evolved during its five-year life," remembers Gregg McCraw. "During the first year, we started to bring in local guest artists. That evolved to regional artists, and then national touring artists. The first was Mary Cutrufello."

"Gregg McCraw's Americana series was just fantastic," recalls Daniel Coston. "I saw so many people that I still listen to through that Tuesday night showcase, many of whom I would not have seen otherwise. Six String Drag, Mercury Dime, Freakwater, Steve Wynn with the Continental Drifters, Mark Olson and Victoria Williams. Deke Dickerson, a photo of which later became the cover of his best-of CD. Alejandro Escovedo's performance in April of 1998 is still one of the best shows I have ever seen in my life. Two guitars, a cello and a violin sounding like an orchestra. As a photographer, you know that you re on to something when you only intend to shoot one roll of film, and proceed to shoot all the film in your bag."

"There were some tremendous shows during those five years," adds McCraw. "The 'Known On The Underground' CD release party. The Drive-By Truckers and Slobberbone on stage together, and the Slobberbone bassplayer hanging from the rafters over the stage. Robbie Fulks energetic destruction of a mic stand during a Michael Jackson cover. Dave Alvin pounding his semi-functional amp during a marathon evening until his rings cut his fingers open, and he left the stage bleeding. That was the same night Todd [Smith] tossed a drunk out the door, and across the hood of my car."

RANK OUTSIDERS, AMERICANA NIGHT'S CELEBRATION OF
THE DOUBLE DOOR INN'S 25TH ANNIVERSERY, DECEMBER 1998.
Photo by Daniel Coston

DAVID CHILDERS, 2000.
Photo by Daniel Coston

ALEJANDRO ESCOVEDO, MAY 1998.
Photo by Daniel Coston

WALTER SALAS-HUMARA, THE SILOS, OCTOBER 1999.
Photo by Daniel Coston

LOU FORD, 1998.
Photo by Daniel Coston

TIFT MERRITT, JUNE 1998.
Photo by Daniel Coston

LEON RUSSELL, MAY 1998.
Photo by Daniel Coston

DRIVE BY TRUCKERS, SOUTHERN ROCK OPERA TOUR, 2001.
Photo by Daniel Coston

Along with the Americana scene, there was a new scene of bands that were bringing in crowds to the Double Door. Popular locals acts such as Lou Ford, and Electro-Luxe (later renamed Come On Thunderchild) filled up the Double Door's calendar, along with shows from the likes of Ronnie Dawson, R. L. Burnside, Leon Russell, Buddy Miles, Levon Helm, and Link Wray, who played two shows at the bar in 1998.

"Link Wray was such a cool guy, and really nice to his fans," says Daniel Coston. "When he came back the second time, I made my way upstairs and gave him my photos from his first Double Door show. Link profusely thanked me for the photos, and told me how great a photographer I was. It really shook my system to have him be so complimentary."

Another local band that attracted a lot of attention throughout the 1990s was the Belmont Playboys, a punk-rockabilly band that brought a different crowd to the Double Door. "A Belmont Playboys show was a full-on event for a lot of people," continues Coston. "Their crowd was predominantly filled with rockabilly fans, who would drink at the front of the stage, and dance behind the soundboard. Some of the best photos I have ever taken of dancers were at Belmont Playboys shows."

The Double Door has continued to draw the best up-and-coming acts in the region. "In 2002, David Childers asked a band he had just met, the Avett Brothers to open for him at the Double Door," adds Coston. "The Avetts had played the Double Door a few times before that, and had even recorded a live album there, but was the first time that many of David's fans had seen or heard of them. Even then, their shows had a lot of energy, and you could just tell that they had something different. A lot of people came to see David that night, but they left talking about the Avetts."

One person that helped capture the live music sound at the Double Door for many years is Les Moore. According to Rob Thorne, "I first saw Les Moore in the early '70s. Back then, Festival in the Park wouldn't let pop or rock musicians play the main stage. So Melvin (Cohen), who ran Reliable Music, set up his own side stage for people to play, and he brought Les Moore in. Les was doing songs off of his two Capricorn Records albums, and he was just incredible. Years later, I met him when he started running sound at the Double Door, and I said that

LES MOORE, 1999.
Photo by Daniel Coston

LINK WRAY, 1998.
Photo by Daniel Coston

R. L. BURNSIDE.
Photo by Daniel Coston

BUDDY MILES, MAY 1999.
Photo by Daniel Coston

LEVON HELM & THE BARN BURNERS, JANUARY 2000.
Photo by Daniel Coston

DAVE ALVIN, DECEMBER 1999.
Photo by Daniel Coston

SETH AVETT, FEBRUARY 2002.
Photo by Daniel Coston

something seemed familiar about him. I finally realized that he was the guy I'd seen at Festival in the Park. Les is just a great guy."

Fortunately, I was able to interview Moore and learn more about the history during the period of the 1990s. According to Moore, "I call New Orleans home, but I came to Charlotte by way of Austin, Texas where my wife attended school. I had played in New Orleans when I was off from my regular job on a towboat. Eventually, we moved to Charlotte when my wife landed a job here. I didn't really play until we had been here for about eight or nine years. I first started playing at Lenny Federal's Open mic night at a place called Ty's. There I met Bobby Donaldson, who helped me get a job playing at the Sunset Lounge. While playing there, I met Jim Brock, Daryle Rice and many other local musicians. So I started thinking that I had accumulated all kinds of equipment over the years so I decided to just load it up and bring it along one night just to see what would happen. We started to attract all sorts of musicians who just wanted to play and my Open Stage evolved from that. I worked at several more venues but eventually, I had a chance to go to work at the Double Door. Nick told me that it didn't matter how many people came out. He wanted to provide the venue and even told me that he would help me unload my truck! It was all about the music for Nick."

Les ran the soundboard and set up the stage for many musicians during his time at the Double Door. To this day, many musicians that return to the Double Door ask how Les is doing. In addition, the bar's famed Monday Nite Allstars came together with his guidance. According to Moore, the original band on Monday nights consisted of Jim Brock on drums, Bobby Donaldson on guitar, Rick Blackwell on bass, Johnny Alexander on horns and myself on guitar. They continue to play each Monday night and have been doing so for nearly 15 years.

The vocalist for the band, Charles Hairston, has been in different bands for most of his adult life. One thing that can be said about Hairston is that he is the ultimate showman. Once he hits the stage, all eyes follow him as he sings, roars, struts, dances and continues until he is perspiring heavily. He is definitely a performer not to be missed. Having a back-up band such as the Allstars does not take anything away, either. Each band member is a professional musician in his own right. Jim Brock, who plays percussion, is a well-known drummer and percussionist. He has toured with several major musicians, as has Rick Blackwell, the band's bass player. Johnny Alexander has played horns since childhood. And by horns,

MONDAY NIGHT ALL-STARS, FALL 1998.
Photo by Daniel Coston

LES MOORE HELPS NICK TO PLAY GUITAR, LATE 1990s.
Courtesy Double Door Inn archives

I mean the flute, soprano sax, alto sax, as well as the baritone sax. One of the most remarkable things about his performances is when he plays two saxophones at the same time in harmony. A real sight to behold! Joe Lindsey plays guitar with an elegance and grace while Chris Allen not only tears up the drum kit, but also pitches in on lead vocals.

Sadly, Charles Hairston passed away in February 2009, after months of battling cancer. A benefit was held to help raise money for his treatment in September 2008 that packed the house. The night was definitely a night that reminded everyone of just how fragile a life can be. The many musicians who turned out in support of this cause showed the best side of the Charlotte live music community.

After the attack on the World Trade Center in September, 2001, many businesses saw a downturn including the Double Door. During the early part of the twenty-first century, Karres was able to keep the business going, many times losing money. His devotion to maintaining the intimate music venue kept him going. One question that I asked him was what advice would he give to any prospective small music venue owners. His answer came very quickly. "First, one should be financially secure for life before you start. And second, don t have any real bad habits. If you expect to do it and get rich, you won't. It s really more of a labor of love than anything."

"On any given night, you can see a show that you'll never forget," says Daniel Coston. "One of the best times I ever had at the Double Door was when Hubert Sumlin came to play in 2006. Hubert was the guitarist for Howlin' Wolf for 24 years, and redefined what a guitar player could do with both blues and rock music. Hubert is also one of the oldest children I have ever met in my life, in that he lives life with this childlike wonder. I wish more people in this world had that sense of excitement.

"Hubert's band for the evening included Bob Margolin, and Willie Smith. Both had played with Muddy Waters at different times, as had Sumlin. As the show began, former Muddy Waters harmonica player Carey Bell walked in and sat down next to the stage. Carey was living at that time with local musician extraordinare Mookie Brill, who accompanied Carey to the gig.

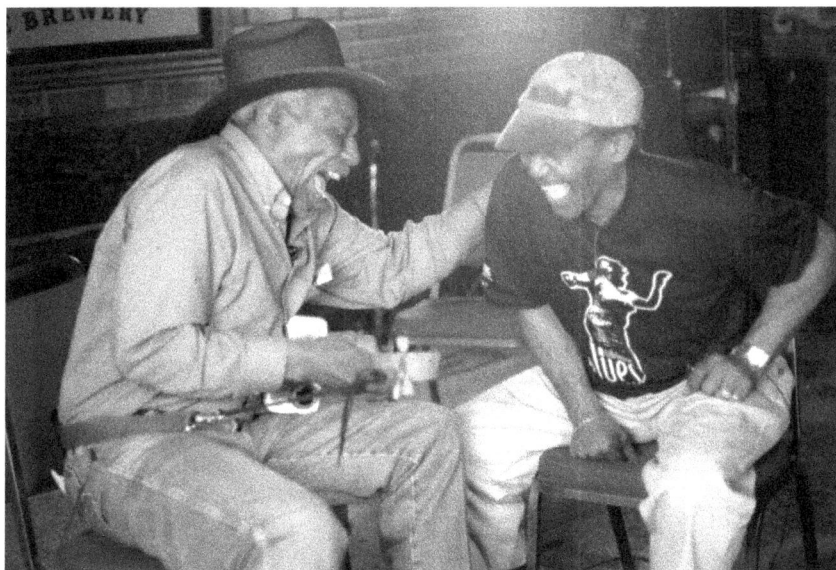

MUDDY WATERS BAND VETERANS MAC ARNOLD (ON LEFT) AND
WILLIE SMITH, JUNE 2006.
Photo by Daniel Coston

(Left to Right) HUBERT SUMLIN, WILLIE SMITH, CAREY BELL,
BOB MARGOLIN, MAY 2006. Photo by Daniel Coston

From the start, everyone wanted to get Carey up on stage to join the band. Everyone except Carey, who sat there and shook his head anytime somebody asked. Mookie got up on stage and played, and Carey didn't move. Hubert even introduced Carey onstage at one point, and Carey just waved Hubert off.

This went on to two sets, albeit two killer sets of music. Somewhere around 1:30am, as the band got ready to play their final numbers, Bob Margolin looks down at Carey and says,"Are you playing, man?" Carey shook his head no. Bob said, "Okay," and starts to turn away, at which point Carey held up his index finger, indicating that he would do one song. Carey had been waiting all night to keep people guessing, and waiting to become the focus of attention. As Bob Margolin began to introduce Carey, Hubert stood onstage and began yelling, 'Yeah! Yeah!' like an excited Little Leaguer. Carey proceeded to play three Muddy Waters songs with the band, four Muddy vets onstage together tearing it up."

Another favorite show of Coston's was Pinetop Perkins' return to the Double Door in 2004. "Pinetop Perkins is another legend that I put up there with Hubert Sumlin. I remember arriving early for his show, only to find him sitting up against the wall, chatting occasionally with fans. Pinetop is so used to fans coming up and wanting to have their photos taken with him, that he couldn't figure out why I was just taking photos of him, and not of Pinetop with other folks around the bar.

"The Pinetop show was also the first time that I saw the legendary Nappy Brown. He came onstage during the middle of the show, and proceeded to roll all over the stage, began to undress while sitting on a woman's lap, and generally took over the building for his twenty-minute slot. There's been so many shows over the past twelve years that I'm so glad I saw. Brian Auger, Sean Costello, Peter Tork. The list is endless."

In November of 2007, Micah Davidson was hired at first to work in the kitchen. Several months before, Davidson had formed an organization dedicated to staging live music shows. The name of the organization is Carolinas Live Music Society. His knowledge of the music business was soon put to good use, as he began to assist Nick in booking bands for the venue. One of Davidson's goals, he shares, is "to try and find good music and bring more people into the Double Door to see different bands. Many of the older Blues acts are no longer touring, but there is an amazing amount of live music available.

BETTYE LAVETTE, 2006.
Photo by Daniel Coston

MICAH IN HIS OFFICE, AUGUST 2008.
Photo by Daniel Coston

Davidson also feels that the Double Door can continue indefinitely with the right blend of music and patrons who will come out to see shows. Although he is only 30 years old, Davidson has learned quickly about some of the problems inherent in remaining in the small bar/music venue business. He feels confident that the new types of music that he is helping book for the club will help insure that the business will go on. "We've got surly bartenders, smoke-filled rooms and incredible music," he says. "I want this to be a place where bands want to play here and be able to say that they have performed on this stage."

Over the years of his employment with the Double Door, Mike Martin has seen many things change. He understands the difficulties involved in running a live music venue in a small bar. Many of the younger people that are starting to come in for shows are not accustomed to paying a cover charge. "I know there has been some controversy among some of our older customers about some of the recent changes in our featured bands. But I really enjoy some of the newer music, says Martin. "The style may be a little different from the conventional blues music that made us famous, but many of the blues stars do not tour as much as they once did. Those who do still tour, often must have financial guarantees to appear at all. That means that we have no choice but to charge at the door. That is a difficult concept for some of our younger customers to accept." Bringing in Micah Davidson to help with the booking duties is a decision that Martin sees as an inevitable part of the change needed to sustain the venue into the 21st century. "Over the past few months, I have heard some really killer bands that Micah has booked," adds Martin.

After having spent the last 40 years in this business, Nick Karres states, "One of the biggest things that I am proud of is what we've accomplished. Not that this has been a huge business success, but I 've always believed in doing the best you can with what you have. This facility was not built for music. It was originally someone's home. But as we got into presenting live music shows, we became a groundbreaking club. I wish I had all of the money that we have lost on bands but we put our money where it counted, by taking chances on bands, having both good nights as well as bad ones. The thing that I am most proud of is just how much we did accomplish. We took the chances, we rolled the dice all the time. I would hope that we have provided good music and good memories for our patrons over the years."

TRACIE LEWIS WORKING BEHIND THE BAR, AUGUST 2008.
Photo by Daniel Coston

TRACY ABERNETHY (ON RIGHT) AND TODD SMITH PREPARE FOR THE
EVENING'S PATRONS, JULY 2008. Photo by Daniel Coston

BEN JOPLIN, LONGTIME MAINTENENCE MAN FOR THE DOUBLE DOOR INN.
Photo by Daniel Coston

NICK KARRES AT THE 35TH YEAR DOUBLE DOOR BOOK-CLOSING PARTY, JUNE 8, 2008. Photo by Daniel Coston

Daniel Coston, who has traveled extensively during his photography career, makes this observation. "It's really when you start traveling elsewhere that you realize how rare a place like the Double Door is. Long-standing watering holes just don't exist in every town anymore, let alone provide music under the same ownership for thirty-five years. More often than not, these places are spots that people reminisce about, telling tired stories of the place that used to be, before the lot was bought up and turned into a shopping mall. The Double Door is the real thing, and it's still here."

Kelly Karres, Nick's daughter, was kind enough to write a piece to be included in this book. She shares her own unique perspective of the business, as seen through her eyes.

KARRES FAMILY, 35TH YEAR DOUBLE DOOR BOOK-CLOSING PARTY, JUNE 8, 2008. Photo by Daniel Coston

"BECAUSE NICK IS MY FATHER, I HAVE A UNIQUE PERSPECTIVE OF THE DOUBLE DOOR. I REMEMBER WALKING INTO THE DOUBLE DOOR WITH MY FATHER ON SATURDAY MORNINGS, WITH WADS ORANGEADE IN MY TINY HANDS. I CAN STILL HEAR THE OLD HARDWOODS CREAKING BENEATH MY FEET AS WE WALKED INTO THE BUILDING. EVEN AS A LITTLE GIRL I SENSED A DISTINCT CONNECTION TO THINGS PAST IN THAT OLD BUILDING. THINGS THAT NOT ONLY EXISTED, BUT STILL EXIST. WITH ITS DARK SHADOWS, LONG STAIRCASES AND TALL CEILINGS, THE HOUSE INVITED MY CURIOSITY. AS I STOOD STILL, THE OLD WALLS SEEMED TO TALK TO ME, TELLING ME A STORY.

"AS A YOUNG GIRL THIS EXPERIENCE MADE ME FEEL VERY SPECIAL, AS IF SOMEONE WAS TELLING ME A SECRET I WASN'T SUPPOSED TO HEAR. NOW THAT I AM OLDER, I UNDERSTAND THAT THOSE VOICES IN THE WALLS BELONG TO MANY DIFFERENT PEOPLE. THEY ARE THE VOICES OF THE FAMILY THAT ONCE CALLED THIS BUILDING HOME. THEY ARE THE VOICES OF EVERY MUSICIAN, PATRON AND WORKER. THEY ARE THE VOICES OF EVERY PERSON WHO HAS ENTERED THAT BUILDING AND, IN SOME WAY, HAS BEEN TOUCHED BY IT.

"THE NEXT TIME YOU WALK INTO THE DOUBLE DOOR, STAY QUIET AND LISTEN TO THE HARDWOODS CREAK BENEATH YOUR FEET. YOU, TOO, MAY BE LUCKY ENOUGH TO HEAR THOSE OLD WALLS TALK."

THE FAMOUS BELL AND HORN BEHIND THE BAR, SOUNDED OFF
WHENEVER SOMEONE TIPS.
Photo by Daniel Coston

THE DOUBLE DOOR INN AT 40
by Daniel Coston

ON A RECENT EVENING, I WALKED OUTSIDE OF THE DOUBLE DOOR AND STOOD IN THE PARKING LOT. I LOOKED AT THE NIGHT SKY, AND THE AREA SURROUNDING THE VENUE. SO MUCH HAS CHANGED SINCE THE DOUBLE DOOR OPENED FORTY YEARS AGO. FOR ONE, MUCH OF THE DOUBLE DOOR'S PARKING LOT DIDN'T EXIST BACK THEN. THAT BELONGED TO THE HEAD SHOP, CHRONOSYNCLAS-TICINFINDIBULUM, THAT SAT NEXT DOOR. DESPITE ALL OF THOSE CHANGES, A NIGHT AT THE DOUBLE DOOR FEELS VERY FAMILIAR. LIKE MANY OTHERS, I HAVE SPENT MANY A NIGHT IN THIS PARK-ING LOT, AND IN THE VENUE. CATCHING UP WITH FRIENDS, LISTEN-ING TO THE MUSIC, HAVING A GOOD TIME. OVER TIME, MANY OF US HAVE COME TO SEE THE DOUBLE DOOR AS MORE THAN JUST AN OLD BUILDING. MORE THAN JUST ONE OF THE OLDEST BLUES VENUES IN THE UNITED STATES, WHICH IT HAS BECOME. IT IS AN OLD FRIEND UNTO ITSELF, AND ONE THAT WILL HOPEFULLY NOT GO AWAY ANYTIME SOON.

When Debby Wallace and I started work on this book in late 2007, the neighborhood around the Double Door was a drastic state of change. Longtime staples of the Elizabeth/Charlottetowne corridor were fading fast. Anderson's Restaurant had just closed. The Athens Restaurant, which had often been the scene of many show "after-parties", was about to be demolished, and Jimmie's Restaurant had already been turned into rubble. Central Piedmont Community College was taking up more and more of the neighborhood. Part of my motivation for the book was to celebrate the venue as a living, breathing entity, before any more change came to the world I knew. Fast-forward to 2013, and the neighborhood has turned itself around. Shops line the blocks along Elizabeth Avenue. It may be forty years since the Double Door opened, but in Charlotte years, that is more like a couple of centuries. But thankfully, the club has weathered all of the changes, and is still open for business.

In the past few years, many of those that were among the best to play the DDI stage have passed away. Hubert Sumlin, Willie Smith, Levon Helm, Buddy Miles, Nappy Brown. Even those that frequented the venue as a co-worker or patron, such as Basil Coston, and Debby Wallace, the original writer of this book, have gone on that greater gig in the sky. But the music, and the venue continues on. Where Charles Hairston once dazzled every Monday night, Shana Blake now leads with the Monday Night All Stars. Bill Hanna plays to jazz fans new and old every Tuesday night. The old groups many change band members, or break up, but new bands come to take their place. Lou Ford fans now come to see the Loudermilks, while the Rank Outsiders faithful come to Gigi Dover & The Big Love, and the Loose Lugnuts.

Eric Clapton has not returned to the Double Door since that fateful show in 1982, but fans can still experience a surprise on any given night. In 2006, Don Dixon booked a Thursday night show at the venue. Dixon truly is one of the founding fathers of modern music in North Carolina, having led Arrogance for many years, and then going on to produce acts as varied as R.E.M., Hootie & The Blowfish, and many others. Don also played the venue's 20th anniversary show with his wife and musical counterpart, Marti Jones, so this show was a welcome return for those who've followed his music.

SAFFIRE: THE UPPITY BLUES BAND, 1996.
Photo by Rita Miller

Don's part for the evening included half of Hootie & The Blowfish. As the show progressed, the rest of Hootie, including singer Darius Rucker, took the stage, and Dixon yielded to the band playing a surprise eight-song set, in the smallest venue that the band had played in some time. There wasn't a long line at the Double Door's lone pay phone, as there was when Clapton showed up. Just lot of happy fans on their cellphones, taking photos, and telling their friends about what they were missing.

There's the night in 2001 that Al Kooper showed up to play with the Monday Night All Stars. A few years ago, Dallas Mavericks owner Mark Cuban showed up at the venue with star center Dirk Nowitski in tow, and both enjoyed the All Stars' set, and posed for photos with fans. AC/DC guitarist Angus Young has often visited the Double Door while on tour, often enjoying the music while being largely unrecognized.

In 2011, Micah Davidson left the Double Door in pursuit of other opportunities. In his place came a familiar face. By 2012, Gregg McCraw had become one of the biggest show promoters in the area, bringing many acts to Charlotte in multiple venues across town. In the past eighteen months, McCraw has brought in a host of established and new acts, re-establishing the reputation that the Double Door had early on as a "turnkey" venue. This has included legends such as Billy Joe Shaver, Ray Wylie Hubbard, Pete Anderson, and more. Recent up-and-coming acts have included Leogun, who played the venue in the summer of 2013 before heading out to open a nationwide tour for Kiss. Other young bands come to the Double Door to play where Clapton and Stevie Ray Vaughn played, and where the Avett Brothers played some of their earliest shows.

Another great event that happened in 2013 was when Pegi Young, wife of Neil Young, played the Double Door on a Tuesday night. Pegi's band was made up of musicians that had also collaborated with her husband. This included Rick Rosas, who joined Neil for a Buffalo Springfield reunion in 2010 and 2011, and the legendary keyboardist and songwriter Spooner Oldham. Walking into the Double Door, and seeing Oldham sitting right in front of me reminded me of how I felt when I turned that corner in years past, and saw so many legends on that stage. Walk in the door, and there they are. Right in front of you, on stage at the Double Door.

PEGI YOUNG, 2013.
Photo by Daniel Coston

LEOGUN, 2013.
Photo by Daniel Coston

In recent years, the Double Door has been recognized nationally as the oldest live venue east of the Mississippi, as well as the Oldest Blues club in the Unites States under original ownership. I am especially proud of that last recognition, for it acknowledges the man that has held the venue together for all these years. On any given afternoon, you can still find Nick behind the bar, serving up drinks, and talking to friends. Much of Nick's family is also still involved with the club, and that familial feeling extends to many of the patrons themselves. Anyone that came to the Double Door in 2013 for raise money for longtime bartender Mike Martin's medical bills, or came to the Spongetones' recent shows can attest to that extended sense of family, and belonging. For many of us that have been coming to the venue for a long time, the Double Door is way more than a club that supports live music. It is a part of our lives.

ON ANY GIVEN NIGHT, WALK INTO THE DOUBLE DOOR. ORDER A BEVERAGE, AND WALK AROUND THE VENUE. LOOK AT THE WALLS, LINED WITH THE PHOTOS OF THOSE WHO HAVE PLAYED THE VENUE OVER THE PAST FORTY YEARS. IN DOING THE ORIGINAL RESEARCH FOR THIS BOOK, I WAS STUNNED BY HOW MANY FAMOUS MUSICIANS THAT HAVE PLAYED THE DOUBLE DOOR DO NOT HAVE THEIR PHOTO ON THE WALL, SIMPLY BECAUSE THERE ISN'T ANY MORE SPACE. ONCE YOU'VE FINISHED LOOKING AT THE PHOTOS, TURN TO THE STAGE AND LISTEN TO THE MUSIC. AND IN DOING SO, THE EXPERIENCE OF A NIGHT AT THE DOUBLE DOOR CONTINUES, FORTY YEARS ON, AND HOPEFULLY, MANY MORE TO GO.

TYLER BRYANT, 2013.
Photo by Daniel Coston

ERIC CLAPTON, DOUBLE DOOR INN, JUNE 24, 1982
WITH THE LEGENDARY BLUES BAND. Jerry Portnoy (harmonica), Pinetop Perkins (piano),
Willie Smith (drums), Calvin "Fuzz" Jones (bass), Peter "HiFi" Ward (guitar).
All Photos by Dillard Richardson.

ERIC CLAPTON, DOUBLE DOOR INN, JUNE 24, 1982
WITH THE LEGENDARY BLUES BAND.
All Photos by Dillard Richardson.

Est. 1973

www.ingramcontent.com/pod-product-compliance
Lightning Source LLC
Chambersburg PA
CBHW060547100426
42742CB00013B/2485